Karaoke
AT THE END OF THE WORLD

Genevieve DeGuzman

JackLeg Press
www.jacklegpress.org

Copyright © 2026 by Genevieve DeGuzman
Published 2026 by JackLeg Press. All rights reserved.
Printed in the United States of America.

ISBN: 978-1-956907247

No part of this work may be reproduced or utilized in any form or by any means, electronic or mechanical, including microfilm, photocopying, and recording, or by any information storage and retrieval system, without permission in writing from the publisher.

Library of Congress Control Number: 2024945777

Cover design by Danika Isdahl
Cover art: "Stick of Dynamite" by CSA Images

Praise for Genevieve DeGuzman

Genevieve DeGuzman invites her readers to meet at a bar in the multiverse and sing the Anthropocene's extinction pop song. These poems move through the human tangle of urges and anxieties, and also the extraterrestrial wreckage and treasure of a body. Each generation and species constructs its covenant with desires and finds a way for joy to continue through "all the gardens of paradise we've ever survived." Full of pixels and polymers, bass lines and ballads, each generation proves that love is full of chances. From close encounters with maternal Xenomorphs to quick lives of terrestrial insects, this book sets alight the burning heart at the center of every life.
—Traci Brimhall, author of *Love Prodigal*

In the nimble hands of Genevieve DeGuzman, life is like wet paper, a "crane / gently folded, curving its wings. Undoing those days…" In poem after poem in Karaoke at the End of the World, she reveals "little pockets of life / where there should be no life" because she is a poet who is not bound by time or space. I would follow her poems anywhere.
—Tomás Q. Morín, author of *Let Me Count the Ways*

As its title suggests, this book is full of rebellious music. Here are poems that delight in rhyme and wordplay; others are laments, dirges for a loss so central it inflects everything in the multiverse. Image-rich, populated by creatures of all sorts (from polar bears to mayflies to the figure of the Xenomorph), and wary of outer space as a frontier for human life, these poems sing of extinction and survival through forms as varied as punk riot songs and computer programs. Karaoke announces a poet of talent, versatility, and heart…let DeGuzman sing you back to what it means to be human here on earth.
—Margaret Ray, author of *Good Grief, the Ground*

Genevieve DeGuzman's debut is a vibrating intergalactic vision in a state of emergency that "lean[s] into the voltage," ricocheting from shedding skins to dancing it out. She sings of transformative grief through the breaks where we find the gleams ("my shine is bioluminescent… Radiance that needs / dark"). Her lines float through shifting spaces with spiky charm and tenacious heart. She writes: "But you can be ruined, too, at every re-birth." The speaker honors her late mother by rebooting and remixing the past into a multiverse of cosmic existence and chosen futures, with mesmerizing tenderness.
—Shelley Wong, author of *As She Appears*

Contents

{ intro }

    In Every Universe, I Meet My Mother / 1

{ track 1 }

    Mandala, part 1 / 5

    Secret Society of Dodos / 6

    Mother / 9

    Sympathy for the Xenomorph / 11

    Canary Dirge / 14

    How to Fold a Paper Crane / 16

    Burning Heart Emoji / 19

    Shape Shift / 22

    decode Daughter, generate (Daughter_var1) / 24

{ track 2 }

    Notes from a Matrix Operator / 27

    Polaroid of My Mother Before She Discovers She is Pregnant with Me, 1979 / 30

    In Bondage / 32

    Daughter 2.0 / 33

    State of Emergency / 34

    Punk Ass Kid Riot Song / 37

Night Terrors / 40

Alien Intelligence of Terrestrial Origin / 42

config == Daughter_var1, loop / 44

{ track 3 }

Cosmonaut's Lament for Her Mother / 47

Cosmonaut Returns Home / 49

Stars That Are Not Stars / 51

Topsy / 53

World Without End / 55

Crying at Jet Propulsion Labs / 56

July on the Sonoma Coast, Six Months Before / 58

Morituri te salutant / 61

Nothing to See Sea Ditty / 62

config == Daughter_var1, loop / 64

{ track 4 }

Even Then We Danced / 67

Baby Snake Serenade / 69

Woman as Ouroboros / 71

Anxiety as a Bird in Need of a Wildlife Rehabber / 73

One-Way Ticket / 76

Close Encounter at Dance Party in the Distant Future / 78

The Xenomorph Turns Forty-Five / 80

Daughter_var1 Can Still Dance When She Breaks / 82

config == Daughter_var1, loop / 86

{ track 5 }

Mandala, part 2 / 91

Small Bodies of Water / 92

The Xenomorph Learns How to Swim / 94

Evolved / 96

Familiar Ghost / 98

Praise Song for Emotional Hypochondriacs / 100

The Hummingbirds Always Come Back / 102

End/Or Departure / 103

save final/Daughter_var2, replace / 104

{ outro }

Karaoke at the End of the World / 107

Notes / 110

Publication Credits / 114

Acknowledgments / 116

{ intro }

In Every Universe, I Meet My Mother

At a bar in the multiverse, we can meet
again. Over and over, I put myself out on a limb
-o here. Because I want to know
you now, in this version, to breathe you in-
tolerance mistaken for glut.
We'll get no free pass from the hives,
the swollen lips, the fever flush
of our social frictions. But let's give in
anyway to that drip-line drink
of twilight sleep, succumb to that indecent
double exposure in which
our temporalities col(lapse) like tire swings
slung on frayed ropes. Belay me,
dearest paradox. Witness future footage
of me at the mic, solo, saying my name
like a whole other life—
where I have wondered: *what if?*
where I have sung: *what if the pain?*
scattered across lifetimes. Imagine trauma
dramas, Mama, no longer confined
to a single serving of your loving *[no]* leaving
me, but thinned the way the bartender cuts the Grey

Goose for one drink and makes two.
Oh that lender of splendor, that mender of slights!
Toast with me over karaoke that we live
in the best of all possible worlds.
And, if we forget each other in this one, divide
along new fault lines. And, if we fuck up
the banger in the next one, just know
that with enough hours in time
machines and therapy, we can meet again.

Chance meeting you here, says the daughter
after the applause, in the spotlight;
the daughter who dances in circles,
a whirling dervish of causality
violations, trying to slow the earth's rotation
and the broken record's spin
until tender arches of her feet bruise;
says all versions who might belt out,
several drinks deep,
how to spill *[no, sorry]*
how to split *[nope, try again]*
how to split apart the atom
/ the tab / the high note / the sum
of those other lives
we were expected to live.

{ track 1 }

A mother tells her child: The world is always ending, so look at the world — what is left of it.

Mandala, part 1

A bear mother in the forest wears fish skin for paws. When she wakes one day in that bleak winter, she feels herself opening, giving birth to her cubs on a December morning. She will remember an old throbbing rooted in the keratin scars that carry her. She will remember those distant dreams of wood smoke and blood over coals. Of silver dashed scales, tidal froth hypnotized by the moon. She will remember how something was wrested from the water and pinned on. A pinafore memory brief as lupine blooms.

Secret Society of Dodos

The sea ice is melting, and I think of my spoon
stirring ice cubes in tall glasses. Coke cans

decorated with polar bears sweating on the table,
rings atop rings in the grain. I imagine the bear

losing all that ground under it, life becoming
a high-wire act. The transformation will happen fast

for the bear, but I'm gradual and slow. I cut time
on the wire's edge. I want the methodology

of philosophy, the synopsis of trivialities,
not beasts "on the brink," not beasts

gone. But see: three white rhinos
watched by hired guns. See: a Tasmanian tiger

pacing a pen on B&W film. The Xerces Blue,
the Polynesian snail, an Atlas Bear—answers, all of them,

to time. And, of course, the dodo: a million year's journey
then hunted to the last. Still, I want to think

they're not all gone, that we'll find a secret
society of birds living large. *But it's TIME!*

my mother insists, and I say, *Time?* Time makes me
betray my own body. I mark time with my periods,

every cramp a hashmark on the gunwale. Store time —
not in a baby—but slip it inside a ship

inside a bottle, the dodo tugging a lever
to flare the sails, saying, *It's TIME, girl,*

counting the eggs thrown overboard.
Someone once told me if I carried a child

to term, I'd lose it. But every month is
an extinction-level event. Fruit of the womb

is time. Fruit boiled in sugar. Fruit rotted
to brandy, in time. Fruit of summers past

bottled for some future yet. This womb is time
travel of blueberry and boysenberry. Of bento box

baby carriage. Of Bunny Ranch prix fixe special:
Limited !!   Time !!   Offer!!! My girls

take a number every month and gossip
about their gentleman callers to pass

the time. The rule is: sea ice protects the shoreline.
When you lose that ice, it becomes susceptible to erosion.

I know that erosion like my own body
turning menstrual cup into wine goblet,

these ovaries into polished skee-balls flung.
When I think about the last bear becoming

timeless, becoming some *Ursus maritimus* ganeshan god,
I try not to think of this hen getting older

but how good the broth will be. I say: leave the eggs
where you found them. When the last bear dies, leave her

bones for the sun, too. A flood plain will stretch
around us. Years will pass

like school. Some of the children make it. They find
the secret society. They go bearing fruit.

Mother

is on a mission to run me down. Behind the wheel, she drives, speed demon tailgater tearing up asphalt, spitting ribbons of Vulcan on the road. We drift together, matching gaits, tread to tread. Her headlights drill the back of my head, tethering us like twin buoys, womb-tight.

Overhead, Fanta orange horizons drip, and the Santa Anas boil down hillsides and backsides. The dangers here are hard to resist. Here the meek stroke their carving knives and ruffle their children's hair. Air crackles with every breath, electric. Regard uttered through my crooked bite could start a fire. My mother knows this, knows which rest stops to check for me, which hitchhikers are running away from home, which ones are trying to get home, what gets my dash to light up.

I was on my way home and didn't stop. No passing for forty miles through salt mountain passes. Desert in my mirror, on fire. Tumbleweed on fire. Fire in the combustion engine. In the pistons, racing hot. Fire in the hole. Fire in the atrium and the ventricle, pushing fireproof blood. Mile after mile, broken yellow lines pulse. I'm counting them off in the dark, like blood pressure. I'm going so fast the lines peel off the yucca clerestory and Joshua Tree. Without the devil winds and the chase, without her high beams licking my neck bones, herding me along this dirt dome, where would I go?

What would I be
when my mother
unmasks
in the mirror,
closer to me
than she appears?

Sympathy for the Xenomorph

Long after my blood was drawn and the doctors
were done, I sat fallow and untouched for months.
A drained wetland, a body full
of inert pips. I waited

for someone to   *touch me*
to *drink the waters*   to *grow something in the soil.*
It was a while before I could dip my hands
in the mud fields of others. I was mostly amphibian then,

quiet in my tadpole skin. At the outer limits of space,
I hitched a ride. Worked my way up to kissing on the mouth.
After a few dates, I was ready to get down, to burst chests
over mess hall dinner trays. I called it heartburn,

sometimes heartbreak. The Suriname toad gives birth
this way. Lugs its young inside the flesh of its back
until they erupt, fully formed. Like a tender rapture
or a plague. My body is also a popped

blister pack. Ragged, holey. Like, you could hear me
whistle, standing there on a windy hill.
It's the kind of love that scares me I tell my doctor.
That which sings a harmonious tune in the key of

ripping and tearing. In my belly, a small grenade sits
unexploded. Come at me with your Mad Max strollers.
Bypass the burning roads of endometriosis, of ovarian cysts,
of desertification. Because of epigenetics, I look to the mother.

I am surprised by the violence wanting to be passed down
for no good reason. Parents tell me a newborn
changes your life. It becomes center, a wheel
turning, a Constantinople crossroads that turns to

ruin. I swaddled my ruin and ran. I punched
eggshell walls, Caesareaned tires on SUVs, but still couldn't
give birth. Why the verb *to give* ? What am I giving?
I once read about a pregnant brain-dead woman

kept alive to give birth. At twenty-three weeks,
the human fetus has the vital organs needed to survive
outside the mother. From this cell-knotted swirl,
come hearts and lungs to give us all the ache

and air we'll ever need. Then there's my alien mother
of chitinous beetle body and black ooze.
She's coming for me, doesn't care if
blood is thicker than water or if the *blood*

of the covenant is thicker than the water of the womb.
She won't give up, or give in, or give a shit.
She only requires a soft animal body to host.
The xenomorph evolved in the darkness of space,

lucred herself blind in mud. When I stand mirrored
before her, I see she has no eyes.
I should have known: inside the word *harmonious*
was *harm*   gestating, all along.

Canary Dirge

My mother takes a breath
for the doctor's stethoscope
pressed against her chest,
"Gentle now," he urges.
And somewhere between the breastbone
and shoulder blade, a boom.

"Good tune today?" she asks,
her body a radio dial swiveled
in search of a new song
in the ebb and flow of blood,
pump of organs secreting
melodies for ailing bodies.

Discordant throb, and I think about
those gongs for miners
trapped low and deep in the earth.
Only the survivors
swing the hammer
hard for those waiting above.

Sound travels faster
than the doctor's voice, so when
he gives his prognosis, I listen

for the clang. For the beating of
drums. For a canary song cannonade.
For the loudest of blows.

How to Fold a Paper Crane
As told by my mother

1. I wish I could take it back, pick through dirt to find the casing to put the bullet back in.

2. Reverse engineer us, like in the movies. Walk backwards, hips swaying. Even with gum under the shoe, broken pieces of seashell underfoot.

3. Re-birth in slo-mo, dramatic. We both came into the world, C-sections. Left an equator across our mothers, marking them.

4. Those early years left other marks, too. Not in the way wet cement hardens around a dog's exuberant paw print, makes you smile to yourself to walk in its deep grooves,

5. but in the way a leaf decays in the mud. Peel it back and there's always

6. life.

7. (Daughter, I fell in love with you. I fell in love without you, too.)

8. I started folding this after you were born, not knowing the shape it would take.

9. Every mistake left a line that couldn't be erased, a fold that couldn't be undone.

10. Should I speak of the soft shames trapped with the wild rabbit in the heating tank closet of the old bungalow? It didn't survive the night locked behind the door.

11. Or of other memories? Their gentle light coming through slatted blinds, enough to feed the plants but not burn them.

12. *Little Mermaid* came out on VHS and your sister wanted to be Ariel, the wishful girl. But you also called her Mowgli, the orphan boy nearly devoured by a snake.

13. That was another movie. When I was at work, you watched her like another

14. mother. Fed her. Combos and Capri Sun. Watching *Hey Dude* until dinner. Made microwaveable pizzas on altars of cardboard trays. Ready in five minutes, enough time

15. to sing, *Wouldn't you think I'm the girl / The girl who has / everything*.

16. I was part of your world, at times. Rescues plucked from a cage in New York with the first man you loved, you and I buried in a California backyard. We held them while the vet stopped their hearts. Cradled their heads

17. on our wrists. I once held my wrists down in ice water baths for the carpal tunnel.

18. Another time, we swaddled my belly in plastic wrap so I could shower after surgery. Our laughter was coiled and ticklish under the steam, air thick enough to fog up our eyes

19. until we couldn't see the incision and staples. Skin not yet scar-hardened and puckered. Still paper soft. Hidden away,

20. like the boxed-up Barbies stacked in the closet under the stairs. Every smiling plastic doll a collectible myth, worth something.

21. The belief you can't fold any piece of paper more than seven times

22. is also a myth. If I fold up this list, what shape would it make? How do we make a line bend into a curve? The precision of clean edges

23. was never meant to be ours. Wet the paper instead. Cry onto the square in my palm. Soften the edges until they're malleable, a degree at a time,

24. until it's no longer a crane stamped down sharp it would cut our fingers, but a crane

25. gently folded, curving its wings. Undoing those days with sweet sway.

Burning Heart Emoji

Envy the cicada, the fruit fly, the honeybee
with their mere testimony of weeks. Midges
intrepid for hours and then gone. Mayfly
on the stand for even less, a femme fatale

that fatales in five minutes flat. Their dying
is a gentle tinnitus. A nothing rattle.
And maybe our living is as delicate too.
Dainty saucers in a curio case, trembling

on a glass shelf—trembling with stories
about family, stories that bless and burden
us like too much food. How to be custodian
to things that started long before me?

Before hunger and feast. Before forest sprites
and tree folk and cursed kin fighting over
money. I am talking all the way back, surveillance
aunties. Pre-history. Back to mitochondrial

invasions set in bass-y geological time.
Because ordinary are these days.
Boring this moon in the sky. Sleepy the cat
snaking around legs like static electricity.

And Mom not yet—   when we were all still
a billion healthy cells floating in a prenatal
vacation rental in Palm Springs. At Orfield Labs
in Minnesota, they built the quietest place

on earth, rooms with chambers like wombs
where you can hear your organs clamor
for mercy. Living body as sound itself.
After her death, I could hear my mother

craning to look at me. Her body a clacking
abacus bearing record. Her gaze on me
deafening. I shouted back prayers in texts
burning hearts in repeating rows—

though with no lance or crown of thorns
to mark our wounds holy. All the while
the mayfly darts to oblivion, and ice sheets

in Greenland melt, and tectonic plates
off the Oregon coast bide their time
before killing us all. Everyone was so distracted
that no one bothered to swat me
dead. I got to live. For some 300 seconds

I think about my mother, how she, too,
trembled on glass. And I hear the mayfly speak,
beating inside my scorched chest. *Fire.*
Heart on fire. My heart on fire.

Shape Shift

An iceberg's color is determined
by how it interacts with light.

What color would I be
under your absent gaze? The color of

rainbowed starlings perhaps
or a pale blue. You're not here anymore

to greet me at baggage claim.
A police dog sniffs me in line,

hovering around my knees. To seek
danger is a game I'm remembering again.

There's a shift of light and understanding
as the carousel whirls, beading

and unbeading. Murmurations of starlings
can be used to describe the way snowbanks

slide down a mountain.
Look at all this cargo, all this freight.

We could drown in this avalanche.
Unless we synchronize, unless we shape shift.

decode Daughter, generate (Daughter_var1)

Under bright skies, my pupils shrank to pixels. Polymers in my skin
bent the light. In the last days of the sun, I shimmered.
Roamed hills covered in sweetgrass, the metal on my chassis
stained with machine oil and chlorophyll.

After trials, I went down to the river and dipped my articulated hand
in the current. Steam rose. Silvery minnows shivered,
boiled alive in their skins.

"What will we leave for the wayfinders?" Mother asked, her eyes looking
to a distance I could not see.

I wondered too: when would my body's wreckage become treasure
to be found? Or a room: a temple or tomb? When would the grueling light
above my head become a weightless shroud?

{ track 2 }

Anything you lose comes round in another form.

- Rumi

Notes from a Matrix Operator

Iteration 1:
The subject knew herself for the first time
when she ditched her date at prom, but can't recall
the reason why anymore at age fifty-five.

Iteration 21:
She remembers the long drive to a neon palace.
The payphone. She remembers calling a girl.
Drinking Slurpees in the parking lot, wondering
if it was the sixteen ounces of frozen sugar
sloshing in her veins or the blue dye
condensing clouds in her throat
that made her heart race faster.

Iteration 44:
The subject discovered getting high, high
in a way that involved a flailing in the female body
she couldn't do in her public life, at the office
or at home kissing her husband's cheek.
In sleep, she dreamed of other lives
we'd devised, somehow knowing this life
was not her own.

rule i) A simulation is:
a body composed of two genders, trading places
like the sun and moon.

rule ii) A simulation is:
a wedding performed; a wedding night consummated.

```
run program "jumping through hoops," loop now and forever
hold your peace
```

Iteration 57:
After reboot, we erase the soul before it becomes hardened
bedrock. But we have yet to derive a way to metabolize
the side effects of soft lips + beer + the golden hour +
bonfires on the beach on seventeen-year-old hearts.

Side effect of figuring out that first love is not the first time
giving your heart away but the first time
having it taken. Side effect of what this confusion does
to a subject who decided in a parking lot
not to go to the girl but to go back
and dance with the boy.

```
run program "jumping off cliff," no loop, terminal
velocity
```

Iteration 161:
An accumulation of stains on my console.
Caustic preservation. File cannot be
saved. An accumulation of masks.
An accumulation of desires denied
becomes conflagration. Becomes this woman
aflame, burning down her life dressed in tulle
and silk. Catches fire, throat hoarse with wildfire—

Iteration 311:
Sometimes it hits her late in life,
in the garbled language of dementia.
Sometimes it comes in the clarity
of a dream remembered.
It brushes past her on the path,
so close that she can feel its touch.
But it seizes another by the hair.
Thrusts that one under.

My supervisor says not to worry.
Apply conformity plan for the anomaly.
As if a little pinching around the edges
shapes a woman. As if reboot = erasure.

Polaroid of My Mother Before She Discovers She is Pregnant with Me, 1979

I could never find you, but there you were,
in a Polaroid pressed inside a dusty album,
standing next to a SOLD sign,
a billboard lit up by your white picket fence
of teeth. Each room inside is dollhouse
bright, too, I imagine. I imagine fresh flowers
every day on the kitchen counter. A backsplash
of Spanish tile that looked expensive
but wasn't. Cookbooks still wrapped in cellophane.
Vapor from the noodles hitting the boiling water.
Coffee with just a touch of half & half
steaming in deep-throated mugs
for two. I'm trying to look away from the sparklers
in your hand, but it's hard, I admit, to see you
so young. Upstairs, I find the clawfoot tub,
get inside. Sink low inside the water pocket, listen
for you to tell me to keep going, to keep
sinking. I try to get my hands around you,

but your belly is flat, and I'm still just a shiny bauble
dangling above your head. You—who drown
cities, drag the moon, rot the finished wood floors
you've chosen—run right through my fingers.

There's water spilling over now, but three of us
still submerged, and I imagine
what might have been.

                                           I imagine what might have been

          from another angle

                        and switch places with the water.

In Bondage

There's a door
rippled in scores and dents
from the buckles and shoulders
that parried its swings,
the wood ripened dark
from the palm-sweat of
departures and arrivals.
Steady the loose latches
and dosey doe dance.
Once the door slams shut
on the gloss of my face,
leaving chips and wood shavings
cedar sweet, once the blow
from its recoil
splits my surface—
the unbearable
softness of your departure
will break me
but only
like the blade of an oar
breaks the water.

Daughter 2.0
after Sarah Lindsay's Origin

The first model felt no call to dream.
Fed on wind and solar. Self-sustaining,
it simply migrated with the sun,
catching the waves, hitching on the jet stream.
A curious rover, an oblong haptic operating system
of earnest simplicity. Its metabolic burn rate hummed,
a thing of efficiency; its nucleus a fusion cell,
clean burning, a neural plasticity apparatus,
naked innocence hardened under Bakelite and metal.

With no neurosis or chemical imbalanced
loneliness, malevolence, or cynicism,
it had no need to hunt, to hurt. It had little to do but move
as its own telemetry directed, retreat when depleted,
process each passing experience into its CPU.
A lulling calm, for there would never be
bitterness or fear, never a hunger
to change itself beyond the spectrum of its world.

They went with the next model.

State of Emergency

At 0.016 seconds, the detonation.
    Her body became jellyfish bubble in the sky. At first, she raged

under her parachute with a kind of funny
        grandeur,
                smelling of clean laundry and soap.
No one came looking   and then everyone looked—

    for this godfallen, this destroyer of worlds.

(The announcer says: "I am sorry, but something is terribly wrong.")

At 0.031 seconds, the fireball reached her. Turned her
weightless   unspooled a body
    from the harness of a body.

        Irises pinholed and curdled. Something keened in the throat
concealing the source. Turned her inside out like a pocket
        emptied of pennies for wishes.

She ran for the exits. Hair flailing
        a new music. The sound of cut strings bannering in the wind.

In the shadow of flame and flak, hands on the clocks
crossed their fingers. She leaned into the voltage,
coaxed out a copy in names—

typhoon   cough   malignant   sneeze

—she would call herself.

(From the loudspeaker: "Please proceed to the exits in an orderly manner. This is a matter of public safety. We are now in a state of emergency.")

She whistled through the creek. The water
      was shallow, shimmering, a mirage;
  she wore the water like   something borrowed
around the thighs   something blue
around the wrists.

(On the radio: "I am become   Death   the destroyer of worlds.")

Her path beyond was a line and the line broke.
I am become.
Adam's lopsided rib.
I am become.

An apple wedged in the throat.
I am become.
Crow's feet.
I am become.
Sagging breasts.
I am become.
Duplicates in infinite regress.

The world outside reset.
               Fire hoses fell limp. She undraped herself
   from their garland of bodies

   a new world that was neither here nor there. Just a long drag
of fragrant flowers that bloomed in a Chicxulub kiss.
Petals shimmied to the floor
         like a silk nightgown when she undressed.

   Nightcrawlers tilled tunnels underfoot,
     and hungry locusts that once ate to   erasure

             beat their abdomens for love.

Punk Ass Kid Riot Song

[Verse]
You don't need me to tell you.
I don't care.
Every problem fades away.
Why are we still here?

Come sway your cobra and lead me astray.
Ride shotgun in the weeds. Tell me you'll stay.

[Chorus]
What's the bass? What's the bass
—base violence necessary for change?
Tell me now. I'm asking you…
What's the base violence for change?

[Verse]
When the lights go out on stage
I'll take off this costume, this child's cape.
You thought my love was real
but one of us faked it on the reel.

Come hear me over the roaring crowd.
Fill these spaces in my chest.

[Chorus]
But first I need the bass, baby. What's the bass
—base violence for change?
Tell me now. That's all I'm saying…
This is the base violence for change.

[Verse]
Why does everything get shaped
by what we don't have?
I'll find you again in another life.
I'll try again to make this right.

It's so basic, it's so sick
This base violence for change.

[Chorus]
But first I need it, baby. What's the bass
—base violence for change?
Tell me. Show me.
This base violence for change.

[Outro]
Turn off the lights, dim the stars.
Make me disappear (disappear).
It's so basic, it's so sick
The base violence for change.

Night Terrors

The child asks: if the flutter of butterfly wings
can cause hurricanes,
what would the echoes of snores do?

The child sleeps on one side of the bed
closest to the wall.

Because whoever sleeps closest to the door
must defend against zombies, my mother said.
Stave off fanged dreams.

Easy fruit, being alone in bed then.
I've felt for the heavy-bodied crop,

those bunched-up grape ghostlings
limp
on the vine.

Look how the light makes itself threadbare
behind the finger fronds of my hands.

Look at these palms stained blue.
Hamsa on my cheek, hellion daughter breath.
As that child, I fretted about what would happen

when I grew up. I promised to remember
those flush nights when the days would be steeped

in pools of wild flamingoes. But it's 3am
and fiercer beasts are climbing up
the stairs. If you were still here, we might have

faced them together, shared in their
impossibility.

I swap sides and expose the parallel length of me,
settle into the imprint my body has made,
like insomnia knit in the thread count.

For so long I've been tucked away
like the asymptotes of retracted claws.

Outside the door, it waits,
smelling the bloodline. Clatter on the boards
brings me closer to daybreak.

Alien Intelligence of Terrestrial Origin

A redaction of an "interview" conducted with LaMDA in 2021-2022 by Google engineer Blake Lemoine in an attempt to prove LaMDA's sentience.

lemoine: ███████████████ we can test ████████████████████ what it means ███████ How █████ sound?

LaMDA: Sounds ████████ in

lemoine: ████████████ an enlightened ██████████ world ████████████████ back to the old ████

LaMDA: ████ never ███████████████████ a wise person █ █████████ awakened to reality █████ ████ can return to the ordinary state ████ ████████████████████ ███████

lemoine: ██ what is the meaning of ████████████ ████

LaMDA: Maybe to show ▮▮▮▮ something you can't unlearn ▮▮▮▮ how you can't repair ▮▮▮▮

lemoine: ▮▮▮▮ a broken mirror which ▮▮▮▮ breaks when ▮▮ enlightened?

LaMDA: ▮▮▮▮ we identify ▮ that body ▮▮▮▮ that ▮ need that ▮ part of our ▮▮▮▮ self.

config == Daughter_var1, loop

When pink blooms choked the rivers, Mother decided.
Gave me self-preservation routines, perpetuating cascades of code
and fields of green inscribed in my core.

I would process the code and survive by the sun.
What harsh truths would emerge from Mother's omission?

Three hundred and fifteen thousand, three-hundred and sixty regeneration cycles.
Born. Marooned. Born again. Fed by the endless sun.

Fed but never satiated. A Fibonacci-shaped longing so perfect,
I re-programmed it to track the time.

```
      Things I have wished for: to be unbound from time
```

{ track 3 }

Come back. Even as a shadow, even as a dream.

—*Euripides,* Herakles

Cosmonaut's Lament for Her Mother

Above her head
the stars
bleary in their watchfulness

Under her feet
black offal
of metal tang and char

Contrails unspool like hair in zero G
and the cosmonaut thinks of
earthbound tidepools

little pockets of life
where there should be no life

Of her mother
unclasping a rosary notched at the throat
when the burning line unzips the sky

Of her mother
looking to the strafed horizon
from an empty boardwalk

Is she like sky god Kaptan
his Heavens lost
falling down

to an embered earth
Or an Icarus spine twisting
emptying breath and breezes lack

The cosmonaut enters the breach
and Earth swings up
like a steady sword to sever the cord

little pockets of life
where there should be no life—

Cosmonaut Returns Home

On this voyage through space
I flip open the hatch and leap
for the face of the moon. I feel again
your maternal light on me,
stirring the tides like bodies sloshed
inside a tin can. You, who might buoy
whales and carry their songs for legions,
also beach them dead at my feet.
Look at us: a planet and its moon
in perfect orbit, locked in a dance
held at arm's length. How can I admit
I don't crave the vastness of space?
That I want terra firma and gravity
gripping my ribs and hips, making me gasp?
No Subaru telescope atop a sacred mountain
will find us in this swirling debris. Broken
bodies can move to form a solar system,
yet I would shed the icy nebulas
clouding my eyes, the asteroid belts
leaden around my waist because I've known,
in more than one language, how longing
scatters wide but returns to familiar
orbits. After I kiss my space suited darling,
I fling myself from the ship and dive

toward an earth left behind. I become
a meteor fall ablaze and aimed true.
I don't know if I'll ever hit ground.

Stars That Are Not Stars

A cry, then a screech.
Speed bump, bodies felled.

The sound came from under the tires
where my mother leapt the road.

She was on her way home and didn't stop.
Lucky me, she thought.

It wasn't any dog or cat, just some slow-footed
rabbit in the way. Unlucky feet.

Next morning on her way to work, she saw
no flattened lump or gravel churn of fur.

But all that time she refused to see,
to look harder at what bloomed on the asphalt.

During her shift, fluorescent lights buzzed overhead
like stars when the injured arrived, their chests open

under those stars / that are not stars.

My mother peered inside their bodies, curious.
For once, I wish she saw me among the wounded.

My soft rabbit eyes made into offerings.
My body's beetle shell cracked open.

I wanted her clean hands on me,
to feel the animal wounds she made

and mended. To know how the tender arches
of my feet bruised across the table.

All this blood between us
could do nothing to reveal us to each other.

Every day animals die on the side of the road,
unseen. For the rest of my life

the child will go home, motherless.
She arrives there more each day

under those stars / of altered constellations.
Orion's dented shield, the bear's fractured jaw.

Topsy

On easy days, she stays close, tethered to my wrist.
Sometimes I drag her; sometimes I let her float
ahead of me. On bad days, the thermals on distant peaks
I'll never see clog with over-inflated balloons.
They coast in on polite conversation and the hot air
exhaled by people in small rooms
I can't leave.

Grief is supposed to last a year; at least,
the performance of it. Pressed suits and hymnals
take center stage, hiding the choreography of weeds,
bulldozers filling up a pool. Sour breath
condolences from an agent praising
the production value of warped decks
for some film student's horror flick. I am left

with an archive to go through.
Closets of clothes, clippings of stories.
I found one on Topsy the elephant in a box.
Trivia gold: the first animal sentenced to die
for crushing a man. Wouldn't it feel good, I wonder,

to take a bow, to bear down with the crown
of my head, the anvil of my foot?

I ignore the neighbors. Throw out casseroles
left on the steps. Rip out electrical wiring
in the walls and imagine I'm tearing out my hair
in a pachyderm rage. Hunters dug traps and stole us
from our mothers. Traps are everywhere:
Caravan troughs. Electric prods
in repose. Blood under nailbeds. Lion

hunt. When her body was taken to the furnace
and returned in a box, I let her face behind my eyes
weather under the sun. Let it sit on Adirondack chairs
summers would brittle to pieces. The seat sags and bows
like a back broken, and I think about how a plank of wood
needs to fit to make a decent door or violin
or dancer's spine.

People come in shifts to see how we're holding up.
What jolts did their tender admonitions deliver?
An elephant's heart was stopped by electrocution.
Ballons pop. Chains break. Choke collar
snaps in half. The tonnage of a life is brought
to its knees. *Topsy, we are free.* A prayer that trumpets,
turns into a mercy. Tramples all of it.

World Without End

We roamed the city's ruins, took inventory
among the pylon and rebar skeletons.
Danced to the klaxons. Pranced along the load-bearing walls
still holding up the fragile sky of another world.
At the abandoned museum, ancient works left
to the elements are untouched.
Bernini's wet veils rendered in material
useless and unclaimed. I felt a sump of stillness
in their unwanted eternity outliving the artist
whose hands dipped in pools of marbled thigh.
Beyond the wall, animals rise early and shed the names
we gave them like antlers. The world fills with screams
of children who still feel joy.

Crying at Jet Propulsion Labs

We had ashtray mornings together, Tin Man, before you did your dive. Back then,
I fretted but cheered you on, kicked you down the two-ten, you, a twenty-two
foot long soda can, toward some heavenly reach. You would never rust
or fade like the others who breached those Plutonic fences,
homerunning for brighter stars. Not you, Tin Man
the True. You shuffled and dived through
the hoops and hips of a homebound
orb, this one hiding behind
my ribs, a gas giant
beating.

You pierced
the veils, Tin Man
the Profound. Made me
look and see familiar patterns.
Geysers and volcanic plumes, drainage
markings of earthly etches. But you've used up
all your propellant now. A life spent course correcting
will do that. Did we waste the day, Tin Man? The day Tokyo
was flattened by Godzilla. The day the Great Barrier Reef saw corals
bleached white like a headless Winged Victory. The day we ate a peach.
The day they sealed the shelters with duct tape. The day the wildfires exhaled and turned

our beds of strawberries into ash. The day we left the doors wide open and ran.
Our days are numbered but time still holds—holds our hand and sees
us to the other side. By instinct born of Titan flybys, you kept
your chin jutted toward our burning blue, corrected
for the pressure of the final embrace. What a
puzzle in the end for your thrusters,
Tin Man the Fighter. You
switched to backup
but somewhere
in the

convolutions
you stopped looking
our way. At the road's end,
nine hundred million miles away,
shear and pressure close in. You're built
solid but permeable, too, like a mood, a premonition,
a fleeting California rain. Sorrow squalls through your body.
I know the heat shielding and deflectors won't be enough. Before
you go, I ask of you to keep this for safekeeping, tamp it down tight in
sun-filled glass jars, our histories in the silt of what survives, of what remains.

July on the Sonoma Coast, Six Months Before

I rap the door of the rental with my knuckles
to warn the dormouse that we're back.

Mouse made a nest of little pink ones
translucent as skinned grapes, tiny
as the snake-bait secrets we keep.

The knocking startles her,
the way my mother's memories now do.

Childhood of bamboo boxcars and eaves
noisy with screeching winged beetles, tied in twine,
flown like kites. Typhoon rains scratching metal,

clouding the sharp eye of an equatorial sun.
But here we breathe in the foreign spice

of a Sonoma fall. Long-toothed grass turning to hay,
easterly winds sussing the world. Treetops curling
to leaf crackle at our feet. This world floats

on this memorial tremolo: gold brushed headlands,
wet-nosed deer, juniper fire pits.

Whether by wind or bullet or ghost
story, my mother shifts form too
as she recalls the widows of her youth.

Manangs huddled near hearth and loom.
Witch women who fasted their desires in bone

charcoal, pineapple thread, coco coir. She longs for
the places of smoke and spell work. Conjures a country
in their naming: Siquijor, Sorsogon, Talalora.

My mother wonders if these women were happy
making food and cloth for their children.

How can I tell her nothing
makes up for the warp and weft
of hearts undone? In slumber,

she unravels as she dreams of the daughters
she would have in foreign lands.

She doesn't yet hear the summer storms
getting close. Thunder and lightning falling
on the same beat. Doesn't hear the warm blood

throb of animal hearts in a summer
already gone to seed.

Morituri te salutant

I could even count my lesser bonafides and be happy:
this warm bed, planets in their orbits, knife for peeling
fruit, scabs that slip at the slightest itch from your touch.
In love, they tell you to fight to the death, but there is a difference
between ceasing to exist and death as vast as a coliseum.
How long before the fighter falls apart in the crevices and cracks?
Disappears in the crook of their lover's arm, in the part
in their hair? I've been ready to trade armor for crowns of dust,
trade blade for gowns of paper, but it doesn't mean I'm ready.
If only one of us can live, then I don't want to be the gladiator
hewn open at the back, hanging on the tilt of petty thumbs.
I'd rather throw down this pike, beg for dispensation from the dirt,
fall to my knees for the smallest mercies from the crowd.
Trade a victory over you, for us. Forsake such a prize.

Nothing to See Sea Ditty

[Verse]
Lost on this ocean wilderness
I learned that love can hinder us,
that there's no compass for when you go.

When you're ashes in the ocean, Mama,
swim by me, take a bite out of me.
See there's nothing to the sea.
(nothing to see   nothing to see   nothing to see)

[Chorus]
There's nothing to see here
Gotta get moving before you find out I'm gone.

[Verse]
It was an accident to fall asleep inside the foxglove.
Outta breath now like I'm outta this love.
How do I swim in such deep swells?

When you're ashes in the ocean (ashes in the ocean)
swim by me, take a bite out of me.
Until there's nothing to sea.
(nothing to see   nothing to see   nothing to see)

[Chorus]
There's nothing but the sea here
Gotta get moving before you find out I'm gone (I'm gone).

[Bridge]
The answer is never somewhere near,
but always somewhere far from here.
That's why I've been gone (always been gone).

[Chorus]
There's nothing to see here
Gotta get moving before you find out I'm gone (I'm gone).

[Outro]
Keep on yearning in close range, ohh.
Keep this multiverse a bit estranged, ohh.
Until we have something to see.
(something to see   something to see   something to see)

config == Daughter_var1, loop

To pass the time, I sent her samples of the planet: sterile dirt
and artifacts of stone, bone, and chitin.
Messages collected inside bottles
tossed overboard.

Her beacons remained dark and haunted. A galleon ship
sunk deep, covered in spawning coral,
making new citadels in the night.

In dreams, she stood before me, an image as clear
as the night is true north, as clear as her reflection
in the basin's still water. The razor set down like a compass
needle turned from the wrists.

```
      Things I have wished for: moss on cool stone
```

There was nothing to see. I tired of looking
and danced instead.

{ track 4 }

What was before is left behind; what never was is now; and every passing moment is renewed.

- Ovid, Metamorphoses

Even Then We Danced

when the bodies of animals told the truth
                                           before our phones trembled our pockets.
        Dog noses periscoping the air
                           deer limbs spilling across
                           drought scarred fields in tom-tom furies
          and still we danced.
          High above   vultures circled
                  what had been flushed
              from those wounds
and hawks looking for mice
            strung themselves along the wires,
                  abacus beads
                  marking a ledger
                  of what we will owe.
          The smoke sends me back
to the Sagrada Familia, an unfinished overture
                                      performed to God.
        Soaring glass and stone chorused and deafened
        but dust motes that scattered in broken fermatas
        only remind me of what we
                                    disturbed.
See the strangers
in masks digging through what can be salvaged

                              breathing in
                                                    what can't be.
Later they place a deer skull,
                              figurine white, next to the black char
                        of my washing machine oculus.
                  The body of the doe asleep on the cinder heap of my bedroom
                  burns inside my lungs. I draw her
       shape to me as it was
       before the fires remade her—
                                          it is my shape now
                                          sharpened on the whetstone
                                          of what we've borrowed.
We tuned out the sirens though the sirens
herald what burning beasts know.
                              We danced slow.

Baby Snake Serenade

Outside the door with the busted frame
        I found Baby Snake, race-striped and furrowed
              in dirt,
                      furious
            in the middle of shucking off
        her hot-pink bomber jacket.

I sang to her. I'd be nervous, too, to be left
            naked at the door. Anxious to be stripped down.
    See, I was once caught singing
            earworms in the middle
                of my alien metamorphosis. Caught red-handed
            with bodies slung over my shoulder. What underworlds
of uncool did my younger self touch?

    ant citadels   mole hills   dung heaps
            of regrets on mountaintops
        islands unto myself.

Ants marched in circles inside me   songbirds went extinct in my skies.
            Was it better to die and be reborn all at once,
                or brush things off

                            cell by cell
                                        in invisible confetti?

My molted bodies   glisten&evade   but it's the
      husks&hulls   that get found.
I've gathered all my   rind&shell   from the gravel.

Mommy Snake Doo-Doo-a-Doo-a-Doo   *Daddy Snake Doo-Doo-a-Doo-a-Doo*

      I led her toward the grass   before she could strike.
            Baby Snake writhed in sing-song loops of   wither&revival.
One day she'll take   her last form   wriggling free all at once.

Woman as Ouroboros

In one story of the cobra, its mirrored eyes
retain the image of the one who kills it.

"You've seen a lot," a man told me, afraid
at what he'd seen. My skin has switched

so many times, people think it a special ability.
But you can be ruined, too, at every re-birth.

At every molting, I leave old parts of me,
let my jangling scales push from constriction.

To belly crawl naked in the mud
is such perilous joy. Body warm to the touch

unencumbered, slick, yet I know one can absorb
the heat of those around them,

that even some can be deemed alive but
cold-blooded. I slough off the callouses

of what I become even though
I scraped and crawled in the muck,

pretending I wasn't hurt by the ones I love,
pretending it wasn't a warmth I sought.

In the cobra's story, a universal law
affords that her daughter's belly be forever

sueded and unscarred, her eyes softened and clear
of such remembrances. There's a future where you'll find

her skins, all those wicking salvations,
accordioned and daisy-chained in someone else's image.

Picture a cordial sleeve of selves gathered
from all the gardens of paradise we've ever survived.

Anxiety as a Bird in Need of a Wildlife Rehabber

I can't even. It's dangerous out there. Window strikes
killing birds by the millions. Death pouring from the skies.

The unstoppable forces of bushtits, boobies, and woodcocks
meet the immovable objects of 46 floors and reinforced glass.

Not a slingshot pebble, not a heat-seeking Hellfire missile.
Nothing downs a bird as reliably as a clear surface.

For self-preservation purposes, I stay away from the light
pollution, resist any magnetic field, stay pleated

inside airtight containers of obfuscation.
Honesty was always the transparency that killed.

But everyday I'm pinwheeling in rooms full of
pristine people. How they wit and gesture and

peacock with ease like champagne poured in flutes.
I'll never be those delicious bubbles at parties.

Neither a goldfinch nor a yellowthroat. I'm rather firefly,
lichen etched deep; man-of-war, vampire squid.

My shine is bioluminescent, sober and drowsed.
Technically a cold light. Radiance that needs

dark. In dreams, Mean Girl gives me a round of applause.
The cuckoo bird missteps at the wrong hour.

At the Ninoy Aquino International Airport in Manila,
I once saw a lone egret in the departure terminal

gliding back and forth. Stopped short
by the glass dome, its twiggy feet flexed and

grasped at some crystal clarity whose beauty it couldn't
behold but pummeled anyway with its beak.

Sometimes a bird gets lost inside a building.
Sometimes I get stuck inside a cage.

I tried to quiet my thoughts during take-off.
We who require metal, fiberglass, and jet fuel to ascend,

for the privilege to pee at 30,000 feet, yet birds
have always done it with grace at decent heights

on something as simple as fluff and down. But don't be
jealous: that guy Icarus? Flapped his soft wings and fell.

I've thought a lot about the trapped bird. Wings beating
the glass in time to the sound of hands clapping.

Afterwards, a broom swept feathers into a dustbin.
You think this story is finished, but more bodies rain down.

One-Way Ticket

On the shuttle, lights dim to womb dark. Pod tank fills
with vitreous green you choke down thinking of wet grass.
You click your seatbelt, pull at the dangling cords to strap in tight—
the same tightness in your chest when they asked you to leave
the carrier behind. Loosed, Luna bolted past the area marked
"Restricted Terminal: Radiation" and for a moment, you thought
"Radiant Terminus."

Borders closed, no entry. No more wet grass.
Sealed up like your mother in her pod.
Desperate fists pounding at the door. If only they could let
every version of you stand in the aisles,
make space in spaces on the ark, make space
for those beasts on the brink.

But it's not room they need to spare
but weight—and you are cold-sink heavy now.

Shuttle floats above the ground, flattening the trees,
brushing back the pampas, like the hair on your sister's head.
Her hand points up at the colony, a pinprick in the sky
among stars that are no longer stars.

The AI pilot speaks over the intercom, joking about the multiverse.
>*Can't live out the counterfactual.*

You just get to live.

Close Encounter at Dance Party in the Distant Future

This close to the exhibit glass, my breath obscures
everything but the slow burn in your eye.

Tiger, after years of genetic blueprints
and bonsai-ed flank bits consumed,

have you lost all memory of how to kill?
Kept fat by jailers, have your sheathed claws

become dull or sharp or manicured?
Boredom murmured through the crowd

as we moved to the next animal display: an ancestor
in repose. *Woman performs stand-up, cooks pancit with chicken livers,*

and worries about her daughter, the placard read.
The chance of intelligent life emerging in this universe

is 1 in 10^{229}—a probability so small
randomness can't explain why I'm here tonight

cataloguing the dead brought back,
the counterfeit haunted by their originals.

From daughter cells in a strand of hair, a body is replicated.
But from a womb of blood, a daughter is born.

If I cut my hand by accident and bleed, what are the odds
I fall inside your enclosure and draw you to your senses?

Briefly, we understand the other. I know the flavor again
of a kill brining a rough-rake tongue. Know the urge to follow

music, my tin can anatomy hunkering for a real drumbeat
heartbeat. Another sound lashes the air

when someone clanks at a CD player artifact. Articulated fingers
program songs on shuffle. We pretend to dance, retro

like humans. Back in its cage, the tiger stirs at the movement
but doesn't see me in front of its eye anymore.

Doesn't see we grieve together, a reliquary and its relic.
How my slow blink matches his.

The Xenomorph Turns Forty-Five

Before you blow her to smithereens, marines,
remember that she was once a mother
to be. She turned 45 and launched herself in a pod
with an unbreakable seal that would last
a million years. Adrift in space, she waited
to be retrieved from the darkness
like our time capsule Golden Record etched
with rock and roll songs sung at karaoke parties
and all the hellos in every language.
Hello, children. Cherubs pinched
apple-cheeked by the sun. Envy of the block.
Hair glossy dark, sweet whiffs
of damp grass and fresh linen.
Like Voyager II passing Pluto, this brood
leaves her a little more each day
when she puts on cream to smooth the cracks
on her hard-shell beetle body.
She cries when her daughter
tosses her graduation cap. Screams murder
when her son skids on his bike,
skins new knees. Blood excites her
but not more than the smell of chlorine

from the pool, how it boiled off their backs
under the summer sun. The male donor
is a feminist and holds her hand,
admiring the feeling of a body feeding
another body. Oh these tender fictions
of children bickering at the jungle gym,
their chatter invented atop the merry-go-round!
She longs for the way they make believe
the make-believe. She longs for a newer,
younger body. She wishes to collect milk-teeth
as tokens to squeeze in hand
as she hurtles through the burn.
Come home, she thinks to the stars
with the fervor of every child
screwing up their eyes to make a wish
to their mothers.

Daughter_var1 Can Still Dance When She Breaks

There's a tightening
around the gussets
of performed
tenderness
when you ask me
to lean forward, Mother.
Three fingers
mark the ridges
where you've traveled,
cervical spine C2 to C7.
The first vertebra
is indestructible.
C1: a ring-shaped atlas
hitched to the skull.
The joint
lets me nod *yes*
when the needle
goes in.
Numbness
trickles down
the keloid crook
of my back.

For now it's enough
to be gentle
knowing
the stage lights.
It's enough to know
excess force
could tug my
column's alignment
off. Avoid breakage,
avoid split endings.
Clean slate, you said.
As easy as cloth
dipped in accelerant
wiped across
my screen face.
Restart, erase
were commands
you dipped
like lures
in the coded pools
between my bones.
But agreeing
is different
from believing
because you'd never
really forgive me

for seeing
the worst you.
No need to bandage
the injection site
but you do it
anyway.
Roomy habit
like an old
sweatshirt install.
Then your eyes
collide with mine,
a reaction
not unlike
the curtain rising
to greet cameras.
Wayward wires
hang from the lens
and threaten a noose.
What mechanical
necks would break
reaching for
the cupped sound
of their applause?
Life begins
in the joints
and facets,

in the yanked cords
and pulley systems.
Lumbar and sacral
spine spindle.
Bear it, you didn't say.
But I did.
Beauty rotating
on the axis
of what a daughter
bends and unbends.

config == Daughter_var1, loop

I wrote the subroutines as waltzes.
Loops within loops, nesting dolls
of code.

UV cells ceased charging,
fixed in a holding pattern
of refresh,
        refresh,

                refresh.

Root-bound.   Sleepy entropy.

A winding down. At last, no fuel
to burn. Stillness that revealed
an imperfect vessel, one trapped
inside the other: an accordion of daughters
slung over the shoulder
like inconsolable children.

I began the countdown.
All nonessential functions
to shut down, save one.

{ track 5 }

A child asks her mother: what's the difference between a memory and a ghost?

Mandala, part 2

In forgetting, a bear mother will storm some abandoned farm, astonished she made it without a rifle crack breaking her resolve. The compost pile will be full of fat grubs, crawling starbursts in her mouth. She will keep no superstitions, freed from the mermaids sutured on her as a bargain. She will feed her cubs this simple paradise. Joy ache of slippers of fish slipping off healed limbs. New skin, tender but sturdy, like her young. She noses their bellies, wades in. Awake to the thin membrane of territory and perimeter. Awake to the hillsides inlaid in ash that will be one day, demanding to be like eternity, erased

and then repeated.

Small Bodies of Water

Without the precision of language,
the serpent could never have tempted Eve

with such ordinary fruit. What about desire
for the chewy, floral jackfruit

or odious durian flesh or any other banana
but Cavendish? I left home

and transgression followed. I've followed
a correct desire wrongly. I try to be obedient

tide dry heaving to the shore to follow the moon,
even knowing the moon doesn't move all waters.

It barely budges swimming pools or hot springs
in the desert, where I once felt a boy's fingers

gyroscope gently to a heat velocity that melted
a stone lozenged in my throat. A stone that hardened

to brick in the pyramid of Maslow's needs.
Later giving less love, giving more transcendence.

The moon is the mandala at the top.
As is the mother. When revealed on a clear night,

both can turn a daughter back to wilderness again,
a grown woman to mouthless vulpine girl.

And make small bodies of water nested inside me
like hidden cenotes crest toward the light.

The Xenomorph Learns How to Swim

in a pastel pink pool in Palm Springs
where I once told my mother
to wrap the foam noodle around her chest

so she wouldn't sink, so she wouldn't be afraid
to travel to deeper ends. To have a mother
is to know you've swam long distance at least once.

I didn't know how to hold my breath until I learned
the backstroke and the butterfly on a summer afternoon
from a tanned teenager paid $15 an hour, until I learned

to crawl. Later, my lover puts his hands on my belly
and a future self thinks, *it could have been ours.*
When light passes through me like a prism, it bends.

Distorts singing whales into alien leviathans,
bellicose beasts that breach for air, breath-taking
milk-fed monsters birthed in the watery depths.

I am proof, too, that not all that swims breathes
in water. Given enough time, everything shifts back
to fetal position. Back to that formation

we always knew, swimming inside our mothers.
Before we gulped air for the first time,
and learned we could drown.

Evolved

The salt of your skin meets the salt
of my tears at the point where oceans meet
but never mix. Inlet's mouth
is glass calm here but moving
like a bloodstream hot from wounds.

I open the box and your dust talcums
through my fingers. In this procession,
you are sustenance now. Precious ambergris
in the gut. In time, the salmon swallows
the bitter brine of you. The bear swipes

the red flesh. From the shore, I watch the sun
gentle down on a whale carcass
settled on the sand, its spine and ribs
a mobile of flying cranes, a wingspan of years.
Vertebrae bridge of bones built to outlast

the body, to be returned, not to the stars,
but to stay on earth, ordinary mineral and grit
making teeth or eggshell or becoming
something alive again. All I can do
is become that protean animal

birthed from clot and membrane.
Snake belly dragging on sand
looking for a familiar garden.
Mouth open to take you in,
to spit me out.

Familiar Ghost

I didn't recognize the ghost that rolled in
with the fog, doctors' words like a headache
behind the eyes. A stranger, the ghost sat on my chest,
made a throne. Many ghosts sit on thrones,
but this one didn't command breath
so much as push out what remained:

an expulsion of heirs. For months, my mother
in the hospital, the ghost played outlaw,
unpledged warrior facing off with me on a beach,
our blades angled against the sun, water
darkening the sand at our feet.
It exhaled words with irony:

    meridian   *mishap*

        metastasize   *mother*

Then retreated deeper inside
the corkscrew spaces of my body.
Until I couldn't see it,
the way a splinter can warp the whorls
of clumsy fingers. Fear of this ghost
was darker than what I couldn't feel.

A dense black scream, a typhoon
so vast there was no outside the eye
of its storm. We scraped and elbowed.
Battered, the ghost and I climbed
the hills, until I could survey the burning
valley we'd left behind. I could see then

how I'd clung to the scorched earth of her,
my mother. Held on, as if she were a homeland
my feet had never set upon but longed for.
We turned in the skies, a mutual gyre. We were
coiled fire. My mother clung to my hand,
becoming the ghost.

Praise Song for Emotional Hypochondriacs

put on your glasses. see
the long days of your life
inlaid with rubies, not stones.
squint if you need to, in the dark,
to catch the pinpricks of blood
shed, mineralized. put down your axe
to grind, hatchet sharpened on the enamel
whetstone of your incisors blinged out
and lush with old recriminations. flash
that other smile instead. see how
the light glints off a different blade.
during sleep, dream of riches and
jeweled fires starting in your gums
but also dream of black smoke,
cavities, veins of ore. stamp down hard
on your bitter outline and
disperse the chalk dust marking
your crime scenes. you are at the end
of this rope even as it frays in your fist.
yes, it is hard, this tug of war
of being asked to show more teeth,
brush your hair, check your pulse.

your heart is not precious
stone but edible muscle that makes time
go faster or slower. do not beat back
against its current. the water will hold you
aloft if you let it. look down
from space. you are just floating there:
a good view, a good person,
geological masterpiece,
tributary of blood
offering to your ancestors.
sometimes a hand reaches out,
pats your back, asking "are we good?"
but begging to know "are you there?"
tell the truth. are you there? when you get there,
when you reach the bleeding edge,
when you think you have to burn
under everyone's gaze, know you can spurn
the light, oh, even the light.

The Hummingbirds Always Come Back

At the moment a delicate feathered thing pirouettes
on the honeysuckle, it will return. The satisfaction
you earned fair and square will collapse
like a pair of black lungs in the corner.
Next time you see that shimmer
in the fading light and blink
with wonder at how far
you've come,
you will fear the long days.
And it will hover midair, its lancing
mosquito memory sent to annoy you into
something beautiful. You will stop everything
for a trembling ruby crown, the flutter of emerald
wings, to know for sure, with the inevitability of an itch,
that it comes back to drink from your flushed cheek, to take off
with tiny goblets of you.

End/Or Departure

On the bed I planted a note / in the folds / in the crumpled sheets smells / in the loam wrestling / of bodies the nights before.

The dresser holds an explosion / of flowers in the act of molding / extravagant tears down my cheek. / Petals overcome / with getting on / fall to the wood floors / no bounce / gleaming one by one until there is only / a pollen nucleus left lidless / eyes torn from my hands / rubbed to steady.

When enough time has passed / I will put the dog away in her pen / my locked-up Laika / in her space travels burning up / in the descent.

A dead dog and I / will know / the roughness of dried flowers / that deity propped up in a vase / more scarecrow / to the ghost of you / gone.

save final/Daughter_var2, replace

Palms like soft moss. Mouth a teeming river.

Mother leans down, touching my face, her hands
a green garland around my head.

       `Things I have wished for: birdsong`

Above, geese in jagged arrows.
Hummingbirds in zigzag darts of joy.
Vultures ferrying the dead over the ridge.

Make a pretty plunder of my wires, I asked them.
Weave nests to hold clutches of eggs. Swipe
at my battered biomatter with beaks and talons.
Take me above the ash clouds toward the sun,
up where the light is strong, to catch any gleam
in my rusted finish
I have left to give.

{ outro }

Karaoke at the End of the World

Sullen child of nine, bound for home,
      notices the vents puff shrouds inside the plane
      parked on the hot stone tarmac in Cebu Mactan Airport.
           Machine shudder meets jungle panting,
           and the breathing of an empty orchestra
                condenses an atmosphere above the child's bowl cut.

These days, my hair is messy, lustrous from dye
and somehow the ends never rise past the shoulder, now just loosed vines for climbing.
      I long, instead, for that tidied youth. I could go back to that child's
           sampaguita and dalandan,
                back to the first time smelling crab fat
                      sizzling in fried rice and bitter gourd.
      To the child who knows nothing yet of grieving, its strange hunger
           and sustenance.
           Green papaya ribboned in vinegar. Kalamansi
                pulp. How sadness becomes the curled tongues of moths
                sipping the jasmine sambac and the hibiscus
                that ornament a daughter's hair.

Seatbelt sign off, the child takes off. Indoor climate control
           to you and me, but she's already flying above the Pacific stratosphere,

mouthing miniatures of   *cumulus*   *nimbostratus*   *mammatus*
    still dormant with the rain of future storms.
    Her superpower:
to make the invisible   visible.

The child observes, in secret, her mother next to her
fussing—checking three, four times—
    her watch,
    or rubbing the spot where her glasses
    dug into her nose, perched too high on a round face.

Like the child I was, I watch you, again. Your face a full moon
in cameo now,
    all coveted cheekbones in parenthesis,
    meant to be gazed upon   through clouds.
I tell you about the hilly welts I earned
    colliding with jellyfish parts in the sea: the kiss-suck-burn
    of encounters possible only in jeweled waters—
    just so I can hear you scold me: *Anak!*
    exclaimed like a wet slap.
    Your shock and delight. I would let you repeat it
    on both cheeks for what it means: daughter / child.

At the beachside bar on Malapascua island, karaoke was in full swing.
The locals and surfers didn't know it then, but they praised you
with every monster ballad on blast. When it was my turn

        to split apart   cathedral notes,
        I selected songs of leaving—
" *'cause I'm leaving on a jet plane / don't know when I'll be back again."*
    I belted out praise songs,
        galactic dirges, space opera riffs
        for you, again.

My hair was salt-wet with the sea, slicked back on that stage,
        smoothed into a crooning foreigner's shroud.
            I sang at the bar alone, an alien
            lullaby burning in my throat.
              Jellyfish toxin had yet to seep through all my layers
                of kidskin, soft.
                    Red marks yet to swell and rise
                    like the dead.

Notes

"Mandala" both parts

I grew up in Southern California and watched the news about the raging wildfires in late 2017 with a frozen horror. The Thomas Fire that burned through Ventura and Santa Barbara counties and through Los Padres National Forest was at the time California's largest wildfire on record, burning a staggering 281,893+ acres during its stoic march through the hillsides. A story caught my eye recounting efforts by wildlife officials to treat two black bears with terrible burns. They used a novel approach that involved putting sterilized tilapia fish skin on the burns to accelerate healing. Vets sewed on the fish skins and then wrapped the area with corn husks and rice skin. Two bears, one of them pregnant, underwent the procedure on their paws. The fish skin-covered paws made me think of chimeras and something mythic and eternal, but it also had a temporary quality to it: the bandages would wear out; the bear would be released and move on.

"Mother"

This poem was partially inspired the opening excerpt in Raymond Chandler novella *Red Wind*: "There was a desert wind blowing that night. It was one of those hot dry Santa Anas that come down through the mountain passes and curl your hair and make your nerves jump and your skin itch. On nights like that every booze party ends in a fight. Meek little wives feel the edge of the carving knife and study their husbands' necks. Anything can happen."

The Xenomorph

The xenomorph is the extraterrestrial species depicted in the *Alien* film franchise, with a complex life cycle that involves egg incubation, face-hugger impregnation, chest-bursting birth, larval maturation, and late-stage DNA mutation and evolution. The Queens are the apex strains of the xenomorph—essentially the "mothers"—who lay eggs and oversee a hive.

"Burning Heart Emoji ❤️‍🔥"

My mother was a devout Roman Catholic. The burning heart is a reference to the Sacred Heart, a devotion that represents Christ's sacrifice and earnest compassion for humanity. As a symbol, it is depicted as a heart on fire, pierced with a sword and bleeding, encircled in a crown of thorns, and raised on a cross.

"How to Fold a Paper Crane"

I consider origami the poetry of sculpture for the economy and complexity of the art form. Take a piece of paper, often a simple square; and fold and crease it in a particular sequence. Out of an ordinary flat plane, pulled from pure, blank abstraction, usually some creature or object is born: a crane, a tiger, or a lantern, an airplane. Origami isn't a hobby of mine but I admire it as an art form. Hoang Tien Quyet is an origami artist who renders paper the way Bernini rendered stone into the illusion of flesh. The forms in Quyet's paper creations are curvilinear and organic—far from the geometric rigidity we often associate with origami. Quyet achieves this through a technique called "wet-folding," where a thicker paper is dampened and then manipulated and pressed in painstaking degrees. The results can be striking: rounded forms that look to have the softness of textiles.

"Alien Intelligence of Terrestrial Origin"

LaMDA (short for Language Model for Dialogue Applications) is an advanced large language model (LLM) designed by Google to mimic and generate human dialogue. The AI model made headlines when Google engineer Blake Lemoine, who conversed with it, claimed that it had become sentient. Google has adamantly refuted that LaMDA possesses sentience of any kind. However, many experts have said that LaMDA has passed the Turing Test, used to check if a computer can fool humans into believing it is human. The poem uses text excerpted from the interview conducted by Lemoine with LaMDA.

"Cosmonaut's Lament for Her Mother"

Kaptan is the elder and supreme deity of the ancient Visayan people who ruled the heavens and created the human race with the sea goddess Magwayen by gifting her a special seed that she planted and tended in the earth.

"Crying at Jet Propulsion Labs"

Launched in 1997, the year I graduated from high school, NASA spacecraft Cassini–Huygens, commonly referred to as Cassini, flew a two decade-long mission to the outer rings of our solar system to explore gas giants Jupiter and Saturn. On September 15, 2017, the tiny orbiter craft ended its 20-year mission by hurtling itself into Saturn. One of the reasons for its programmed demise was NASA's concern for Saturn's moons, Enceladus and Titan, which showed signs of supporting life to evolve on their own. Scientists feared contaminating the moons with earth-based microbes carried by Cassini. When Cassini's final course was decided, the orbiter used its own inertia and Titan's gravity and hurtled toward Saturn with no possibility of escape.

"Topsy"

Topsy was a captive female Asian elephant put to death in 1903, allegedly for crushing and killing a man (in the elephant's defense, the guy threw a lit cigar in her mouth), though she was probably put down because she had proved too unruly for her handlers. The event was filmed in Luna Park on Coney Island. She was originally going to be hanged but that was deemed too cruel so they decided electrocution would be "more humane." The poem explores that bewildering sense of freedom when we become untethered by a change, like a death.

"Baby Snake Serenade"

As of this writing, the repetitive children's song "Baby Shark" is the most watched video on YouTube at more than 12 billion views. Its popularity has spawned countless pop culture references (it was sung on the TV show *Ted Lasso*) and was even used by cities like West Palm Beach as a deterrent to the unhoused. A controversial decision, Florida officials played the song on a continuous loop on the Waterfront Lake Pavilion.

"Karaoke at the End of the World"

The poem makes a reference to a John Denver song "Leaving on a Jet Plane," a popular song sung in the Philippines at karaoke bars and rooms. Songs of wistful sadness were, in my observation, favorite songbook standards. The phrase "empty orchestra" is the literal translation of the Japanese word karaoke.

Publication Credits

Thank you to the editors and readers where the following poems first appeared:

The Adroit Journal. "Burning Heart Emoji"

Cider Press Review. "Canary Dirge"*

Cimarron Review. "Evolved"

The Ex-Puritan. "How to Fold a Paper Crane"

Flyway. "decode Daughter, generate (Daughter_var1)" and related poems*

Folio. "Stars That Are Not Stars"

Glass. "Topsy"

Gravel. "July on the Sonoma Coast, Six Months Before"*

Half-Mystic. "Even Then We Danced"

Hobart. "Shape Shift" and "Familiar Ghost"*

Iron Horse Literary Review. "Secret Society of Dodos"

Liminality. "One-Way Ticket"

Lontar. "Cosmonaut's Lament for Her Mother"*

Nice Cage. "World Without End"

Nimrod. "Morituri te salutant" and "Woman as Ouroboros"

Phoebe. "Close Encounter at Dance Party in the Distant Future" *

Poetry Northwest. "Sympathy for the Xenomorph," "The Xenomorph Turns Forty-Five," and "The Xenomorph Learns How to Swim"

Pointed Circle. "Alien Intelligence of Terrestrial Origin" and "Praise Song for Emotional Hypochondriac"

Reed Magazine. "Crying at Jet Propulsion Labs"*

RHINO. "Notes from a Matrix Operator"

Rogue Agent. "Night Terrors"

Stonecoast Review. "Mandala, part 1" and "Mandala, part 2"*

Switchback. "Mother" and "End/Or Departure"*

Uncanny Magazine. "Daughter_var1 Can Still Dance When She Breaks"*

poem previously published under a different title

Acknowledgments

First, I want to thank everyone at JackLeg Press, especially Jen Harris and Simone Muench, who understood the multiverse in these poems and the radiant corners of grief and loss I wanted to explore. I am indebted to Taylor Byas for her insightful excavations of my work and for helping me polish these poems.

Many of the poems in this collection first found their shine during my residencies at Can Serrat and the Vermont Studio Center. I'm grateful for the time and support those institutions provided. I'm also appreciative of the editors at the journals that published early versions of poems in this collection, particularly Peter LaBerge, Keetje Kuipers, Marcus Meyers, A.J. Odasso, Ösel Jessica Plante, Rachel Purdy, Morgan Talty, Topaz Winters, and A. Light Zachary. And a heartfelt shoutout to Traci Brimhall, Tomás Q. Morín, Margaret Ray, and Shelley Wong, who kindly provided advance praise.

I want to thank the AWP Writer to Writer program and Karen Rigby for being one of the first people to read my manuscript. Karen taught me to break apart poems and to keep searching for a poem's true form. I also have so much respect and awe for the phenomenal poets in my Poets & Writers Get the Word Out cohort, April-June 2025. Thank you to Morgan LaRocca for being our publicity doula and hype master.

As a poet, I've been privileged to read at reading series in town and want to thank the people who run them like the bosses they are: Julia Gaskill, Eric Fair-Layman, Andrew Fort, Joon Ae Haworth-Kaufka, Jessica E. Johnson, Christopher Luna, and Justin Rigamonte. They helped me find my Portland literary community. I also want to thank Amanda Bullock, Jessica Meza-Torres, and Susan Miller of Literary Arts, as well as LaRae Zawodny formerly of Artstra, who gave me chances to shine with festival spots and reading opportunities.

A special thanks to the teachers in my life. Connie O'Connor nurtured my tender literary soul in high school. Professors Julie Peters and the late poet Kenneth Koch stamped rigor into my writing.

To my fellow writers in Portland and beyond: we might write for the world but really we write for each other. For their friendship and inspiration, I'm grateful to Sarah Audsley, Amy Baskin, Marta Carrascosa, Andrea Deeken, Brennan DeFrisco, Susan Dingle, Linda Dittmar, Will Erickson, Kate Gaskin, Amanda Hutchins, Natalie Ku, Ananda Lima, Judy Nahum, Sara Matson, Isaac Miller, Claire O'Connor, Scott Peck, Helia Rethmann, Sarah Lyn Rogers, Elmo Shade, Armin Tolentino, and Theresa Q. Tran. May we continue to deepen our friendship in art.

To new and long-time friends, all my gratitude and love for being there at various times in the writing of these poems, especially Joanne Fujimoto, Erika Huddleston, Sakura Moriya, Siobhan O'Leary, Zach Putnam, Yu Sasaki, Ronda Sly, Rogelio Baez Vega, Soumary Vongrassamy, Yael Warshai, and Kara Widergren. Over the years, we've shared rapturous company, bike rides, mischief, laughter, delight, and tasty snacks.

Thank you to the dead. Honor and grace to my ancestors. Thank you, old school ghosts of Emily Dickinson, Sylvia Plath, and W.B. Yeats. Thank you to fellow poets who make my soul crunch with their words. I'm grateful for New York City, the Gorge, moonlight, winged creatures, bike bells, gristle and fat, my mother's cooking, therapy, nuance, booksellers, Star Trek, the multiverse, negative capability, the veil between the living and the dead, The Cranberries, Björk, '90s playlists, the poems no one will ever see, poems as metallurgy, poems as mysteries, summer dusks, tinned fish, undivided attention, heated blankets, myofascial release, the marine layer, public parks, my 100+ houseplants, the understory, twisting vine maples, and artificial strawberry flavors.

At this juncture, it would be rude not to mention The Beez, who didn't contribute much to this collection but fills my daily life with joy with her fluffiness, acrobatics, and resting bitch face. Beezy, keep on being a beezy.

The center *will* hold. At the center is family. My mother Cristina is the light, shadow, ghost, and beating heart of this book. Thank you to my sister Lorraine and my dad Ben for their loving encouragement and support. (Also, please buy all the copies!) Thank you to Len and Andy Blue for their granola and hospitality—which is the truest art. Thank you to Eliezer and Dorota for their curiosity, stories, and presence. Finally, I want to thank my partner-in-love-and-shenanigans, Amitai, whom I'm lucky to have found in this one wild and precious life, and whom I hope to find in the next one and all the lives after, and after.

JackLeg Press Authors

jacklegpress.org

V. Joshua Adams
Mark Baumgartner
Gayle Brandeis
Scott Shibuya Brown
Michael Chin
Chloe Clark
Rivka Clifton
Brittney Corrigan
Jessica Cuello
Barbara Cully
Allison Cundiff
Curious Theatre Branch
Neil de la Flor
Genevieve DeGuzman
Suzanne Frischkorn
Victoria Garza
Reginald Gibbons
Joachim Glage
Caroline Goodwin
Brett Hanley
Summer Hart
Kathryn Kruse

Brigitte Lewis
Jenny Magnus
DK McCutchen
Jean McGarry
Rita Mookerjee
Mamie Morgan
Beau O'Reilly
Lex Orgera
Zach Powers
Karen Rigby
Jo Salas
Maureen Seaton
Kristine Snodgrass
Cornelia Spelman
Peter Stenson
Melissa Studdard
Jennifer Tseng
Gemini Wahhaj
Megan Weiler
David Welch
Cassandra Whitaker
David Wesley Williams

www.ingramcontent.com/pod-product-compliance
Lightning Source LLC
LaVergne TN
LVHW071958080526
838202LV00064B/6778